WHAT WE STAND FOR

EVERYONE IS EQUAL

the kids' book of
TOLERANCE

ANDERS HANSON

CONSULTING EDITOR, DIANE CRAIG, M.A./READING SPECIALIST

Super Sandcastle

An Imprint of Abdo Publishing
www.abdopublishing.com

visit us at www.abdopublishing.com

Published by Abdo Publishing, a division of ABDO, PO Box 398166, Minneapolis, Minnesota 55439.
Copyright © 2015 by Abdo Consulting Group, Inc. International copyrights reserved in all countries.
No part of this book may be reproduced in any form without written permission from the publisher.
Super SandCastle™ is a trademark and logo of Abdo Publishing.

Printed in the United States of America, North Mankato, Minnesota
062014
092014

THIS BOOK CONTAINS
RECYCLED MATERIALS

Editor: Liz Salzmann
Content Developer: Nancy Tuminelly
Cover and Interior Design and Production: Anders Hanson, Mighty Media, Inc.
Photo Credits: Shutterstock

Library of Congress Cataloging-in-Publication Data

Hanson, Anders, 1980-
  Everyone is equal : the kids' book of tolerance / Anders Hanson ; Consulting Editor, Diane Craig, M.A.,
Reading Specialist.
     pages cm. -- (What we stand for)
  ISBN 978-1-62403-293-6
1. Toleration--Juvenile literature. 2. Equality--Juvenile literature. 3. Discrimination--Juvenile literature. I.
Title.
  HM1271.H377 2015
  305--dc23
                            2013041842

Super SandCastle™ books are created by a team of professional educators, reading specialists, and
content developers around five essential components—phonemic awareness, phonics, vocabulary, text
comprehension, and fluency—to assist young readers as they develop reading skills and strategies and
increase their general knowledge. All books are written, reviewed, and leveled for guided reading, early
reading intervention, and Accelerated Reader® programs for use in shared, guided, and independent
reading and writing activities to support a balanced approach to literacy instruction.

CONTENTS

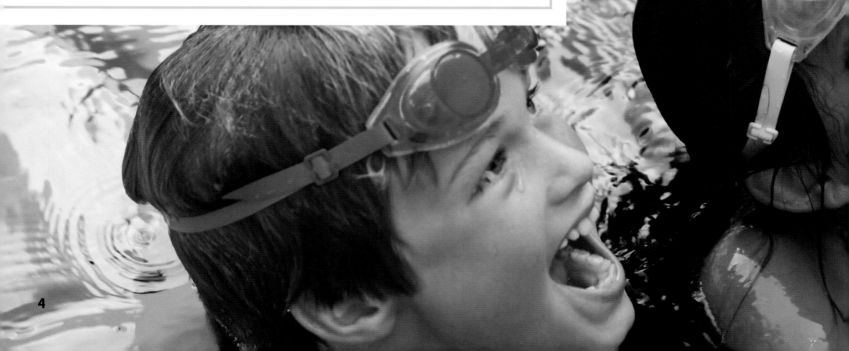

WHAT IS
TOLERANCE?

Tolerance means accepting people for who they are.

Max, Sadie, and Lucy play together in the pool.

5

Everybody is a little bit different.

But we are all human.

Ms. Garcia's students are excited. The class is going on a field trip.

It's good to accept our differences. It's even better to **celebrate** them!

Life would be boring if everyone was the same.

Tolerance makes peace possible.

Without tolerance, everyone would fight all the time!

WHAT CAN YOU DO?

How can you
be more **tolerant**?

BE TOLERANT OF HOW OTHERS LOOK.

Someone may dress differently than you. Or someone may have a different skin color. Don't judge people because of how they look.

BE TOLERANT OF OTHERS' ABILITIES.

Not everybody has the same **abilities**. Some people learn slowly. Other people can't do certain things. Don't judge them. Try being nice!

Andrea helps Gaby learn to count.

15

BE TOLERANT OF OTHERS' BELIEFS.

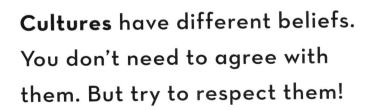

Cultures have different beliefs. You don't need to agree with them. But try to respect them!

IT'S OKAY TO TALK ABOUT DIFFERENCES.

If you have a question, ask the person directly. Get to know each other!

Carrie asked Jillian about her wheelchair. Now they are good friends.

LEARN MORE ABOUT OUR DIFFERENCES.

Intolerance is often caused by fear of the unknown. Learn about the ways people are different. It will help you be more **tolerant**!

WHAT WILL YOU DO?

What is one thing you can do to be more **tolerant**?

GLOSSARY

ABILITY – the skill or power to do something.

CELEBRATE – to enjoy or be happy about something.

CULTURE – the ideas, traditions, art, and behaviors of a group of people.

INTOLERANCE – not being willing or able to accept people different from ourselves.

TOLERANCE – the ability to be accepting of people different from ourselves.

TOLERANT – showing respect for or acceptance of behaviors or beliefs that are different from your own.